Killer History

Why do they leave all the fun stuff out of the history books?

Marek McKenna

Edna Brady Enterprises, LLC
Durham, North Carolina

Killer History: Why do they leave all the fun stuff out of the history books?

For information, address Edna Brady Enterprises, LLC, PO Box 73084, Durham, North Carolina, 27722.

www.killerhistory.com
Print edition ISBN: 978-0-9850482-0-4

First edition: May 2012

For Kim

Contents

Preface 11

Saint Euplius 15

Third in Flight 17

Too Obscene for Jesus 19

Evita! 23

Most Missingest Man in America 27

Sex Scandals in South Carolina 33

Black Bart 37

Lift your Glass to Sam 39

Oy Vey! The Red Coats Are Coming! 41

A Revolutionary Pain in the Neck 45

Hitler's Bloodless Coup 48

Bataan Death March 52

What Were They Thinking? 56

Ike's Dykes 62

The Living Unknown Soldier 65

Sugar Momma of the Country 67

The Gospel According to TJ 72

Presidential Beat Down 77

Hey Big Spender! 91

First American Woman Presidential Candidate 97

Whiskey Ring 109

Grant's All You Can Eat..113

Grant's Tomb...117

Who's your Daddy? 121

Grover's Rules..125

Commander-in-Chief and Head Traffic Cop 127

Unladylike Tactics 131

The First Black President? 135

Presiding While Drunk 139

Afterward 143

"The past is useless. That explains why it is past."

Wright Morris

"History... is indeed little more than the register of the crimes, follies, and misfortunes of mankind."

Edward Gibbon

"History... is a nightmare from which I am trying to awake."

James Joyce

"The study of history is the best medicine for a sick mind; for in history you have a record of the infinite variety of human experience plainly set out for all to see; and in that record you can find yourself and your country both examples and warnings; fine things to take as models, base things rotten through and through, to avoid."

Livy

"History is more or less bunk."

Henry Ford

"Every past is worth condemning."

Friedrich Nietzsche

Preface

Since January 2000, I have guided adult college students through their required history courses. In my work with this challenging group of students, I have noticed that they fall into two categories in regards to their enrollment in my classes: They either love history or hate it. Despite these polar opposite positions for both groups, the study of history will not always be what they expect.

For the so-called history *buffs,* they will be confronted with information that forces them out of their preconceived ideas about the past. For the historical haters, they often report that they have a newfound appreciation for the past because of taking my class. The historical haters report to their astonishment that history is not all about memorizing dates, but is actually interesting. In order to achieve success, both groups must keep an open mind, which I confess can be trying at times.

My job then is to make history interesting, to share the quirks and shortcomings of the historical players. I will from time to time be forced to knock historical figures off their pedestals.

While it is a bit cliché to say, we often forget that the individuals chiseled on Mount Rushmore or that adorn the pages of our history texts did indeed put their pants on one leg at a time. Many of them overate, drank too much, chased women they were not married to, became overwhelmed by their own insecurity, went to the bathroom, and told off-color jokes.

Whenever I hear someone lament about the *good old days* I tend to wince in disbelief. While the stories our grandparents told us about when they grew up certainly might seem charming, and even a tad romantic, the reality might not have been as great as grandpa's memory. Memory is not foolproof: What one participant swears happened another might not even recollect.

One of my favorite things about history is sifting through all the different versions in order to find out what really happened. I perhaps was exposed to this at an early age. My maternal and paternal grandmothers grew up as neighbors and often enjoyed many childhood adventures. They along with my maternal grandfather were classmates. As a kid, I loved hearing their stories about what it was like to grow up in rural Iowa in the 1920s.

As I listened to these stories, I quickly realized that my grandparents did not remember things the same way. Perhaps my career as a historian was born there as I sat around the kitchen table eating cookies and trying to deduce what really happened when my grandmothers separately told me that when they were my age they had skipped school and went fishing.

Since my cigar-smoking granny had actually taken me fishing, I could more easily imagine her bolting for the creek with her pole. On the other hand, she was a schoolteacher, and at my tender age I could not imagine any of my teachers skipping school. I had an even harder time bending my brain around the vision that my other granny who was very religious would partake in this type of childhood adventure.

Over milk and cookies, the historical skeptic was born as I tried to consolidate the image of two old women with a story that just seemed too out of character.

As I learned more about history, the *good old days* hardly seemed appealing. Life in historical times was often brutal, challenging, and even in the best possible life simply difficult. These historical times were especially difficult for outsiders, minorities and for women. To put it more directly, the *good old days* were misogynistic, racist, and violent.

One such ritual practiced by colonial Americans of the 1600s made my skin crawl when I first learned of it. This was the practice of 'smock' or 'shift' marriages. Before we get to this disgusting practice, I should explain the nature of colonial property rights. Basically, the rule was very simple: women could not own property

Now here was the problem, women often outlived their husbands. There were many more women available for marriage then men. When a husband died, if the widow was childless or her children were not old enough to inherit their father's property, the wife was left scrambling to find a replacement husband in order to protect her home and to ensure the welfare of her children.

This leads to another problem for early Americans. Since this was a new country, many families were land rich, but cash poor. Often times, the deceased husband might have possessed a sizable debt, but he might have owned a big farm worth much more than the debt. When a widow remarried, the new husband took over the property, but also assumed the former husband's debt.

Of course, no one wants to assume someone else's debt, so the colonial government set up an early form of bankruptcy relief in the form of the previously mentioned 'smock' or 'shift' marriage. Here is the deal: The widow could wipe the slate clean by eliminating the deceased husband's debt so she could enter the new marriage free and clear. The catch was she had to invite all the bill collectors to the wedding and she was required to wear a thin shift dress to the ceremony. Yes, you are correct to assume that these thin shifts were see-through and the bride was nearly nude.

Basically, the wedding was a peep show for the creditors. Of course, since the law simply stipulated that the thin garment be worn during the ceremony and did not make any other requirements, as time progressed the colonial widows became creative in how they skirted the letter of the law. One story goes that a bride crouched in the corner by the hearth and another stayed in a closet during the ceremony. One inventive 18th century bride took her vows in the dead of night on the top of a tall ladder. She then dressed and came down the ladder.

I think we can all agree that this is one custom we are pleased to not see survive into modern times.

I was recently asked, "Do you ever get tired of talking about history?"

"Well, no," I replied, as if the question was not something I had even considered possible. From my seat, history is the culmination of the human experience. History records our victories, our losses, our pain, and our happiness. As I tell my students, history is about sex, money, and power... and not necessarily in that order. *Who could get tired of that?*

In the following pages, I share of a few of my favorite stories of presidential quirkiness, outlandish scandals, disgusting criminals, and historical figures acting human. I hope they make you smile!

Saint Euplius

On April 29, 304, the Romans chopped off the head of Saint Euplius.

Good old Euplius lived in Catania, Sicily and the story goes that wherever he went he had the gospel tucked under his arm and with all the swagger of a Sicilian wise guy would pontificate to the pagans about the benefits of Christianity.

One day as he preached, a big crowd formed and this got the attention of the Roman officials. He was arrested and brought to the local governor for interrogation. The governor asked Euplius to read a passage of the book and so he obliged. Euplius read the story of Jesus' crucifixion. When Euplius finished the story, the governor asked, "So let me get this straight, before the story gets off the ground, the hero gets trashed without actually making any enemies, then his homies don't try to get revenge, but instead they make the circuit and bore people with the tale of a guy that didn't bust any heads?" You may also be surprised that the Roman governor was such a gangster. The governor continued, "Forget about it! With such a boring story you shouldn't have any beef if we destroy this little book, eh?"

Euplius replied, "Yo, man. Do what you want; I have the book memorized." Euplius was also a wise guy.

So the Roman governor gave Euplius an attitude adjustment, which meant some major torture, then threw him in jail. Euplius was all gimped up from the beatings, but he forced himself to do some heavy duty praying. Let me be clear, the prayer was so powerful that a spring of water erupted in the prison cell.

Now, you can say Euplius caused this to happen through the power of his mind. Another version of the story could be that God provided water for Euplius to drink, as he was thirsty and injured. Still another version could be that the Romans just had crappy plumbing. But whatever you call it, the story looks somewhat miraculous from where I am sitting. Of course, the Romans were not impressed that a little Sicilian dude had flooded their prison, so they put him on trial again.

At this second trial, Euplius was still full of Sicilian swagger and again pronounced his faith in Christianity. The Roman governor still was not willing to give Euplius any love, and ordered that first his ears be torn off and then he should have his head wacked off. Ok, first reaction—a big ouch to the ears being torn off, but come on, the beheading seemed like overkill.

The martyr Euplius became Saint Number 1183, which makes one wonder about what the previous 1182 did to get sainted.

Third in Flight

The Wright Brothers' not so historic flight

I begin this book with a story that may harm North Carolina pride. I have no qualms about setting the record straight, but I am worried about bankrupting the state coffers of North Carolina. If this story gets out, we are going to need to change the license plates. OK, here it is: Sorry fellow Tar Heels, the Wright Brothers were not the first in flight. If truth be told, while the Wright Boys were making their wobbly flight off the dunes of Kills Devil Hills, someone else had already flown a fixed wing plane seven miles, at an altitude of 200 feet. Which makes the Wrights' little flight look just plain wimpy.

The real pioneer of aviation was a German immigrant named Gustave Whitehead, making his historic flight in

Bridgeport, CT on August 14, 1901—yeah that is 28 months before Orville and Wilbur got it off the ground. In fact, there is also strong evidence that the Wrights were not even the second fixed wing fliers.

So why does FIRST IN FLIGHT grace the North Carolina license plates and not the Connecticut plates? It really all boils down to the classic tale of American self-promotion. The Wright Brothers knew how to work the press and Mr. Whitehead was more concerned with wind shear and the physics of flight. It might also be important to note that Whitehead did not speak English so he could hardly be blamed for not being able to give a good interview. It also never dawned on him to hire a photographer to record his flights.

Also taking flight before the Wrights was a craft built by Pastor Burrell Cannon, who aspired to replicate the biblical flying machine described in the book of Ezekiel. In 1902, a nice sized crowd witnessed the successful flight of the Ezekiel Airship in Pittsburg, Texas. Of course, the good reverend also repeated the mistake Whitehead made. A mistake the Wrights would not commit—they brought a camera. And as a result, North Carolina is the First in Flight, which has a much better ring to it than Third in Flight.

Too Obscene for Jesus

Gilles de Rais was a 15th century French nobleman, a Renaissance man, a linguist, a skilled warrior, and an associate of Joan of Arc. He was a devout Catholic and financed the construction of several Catholic churches in rural France. He was also one of the earliest known serial killers on record.

De Rais' blood thirst began when he was a soldier, and after his retirement from military service in 1435, at the age of 31 he grew bored bumping around his big castle. While on his travels he encountered what the historical record called, a 'pretty boy' named Poitou and invited him back to the castle. Poitou was brutally raped by de Rais and was spared from being murdered when a servant suggested keeping him around as a page. Putting his big sword back in his scabbard, de Rais spared the pretty boy's life, and in return Poitou became one of his most devoted servants.

Of course, this was just the beginning of de Rais' brutality. Over the next decade, it is estimated that he raped and killed as many as 200 children all with the assistance of his servants. The kids were lured to the castle under the guise of work, money, clothing, or the offer of a hot meal.

Once inside the privacy of the castle, they were secured on a rape stand where de Rais got his perverted kicks by repeatedly raping the boys. Finally, either de Rais or one of the servants would decapitate the kid. De Rais would then retire to his bedroom as the servants cleaned up the bloody mess.

Eventually de Rais went too far when he kidnapped a priest, which in France was a capital offense. Somehow, the priest was able to escape and alerted the authorities. Gilles de Rais was arrested and tried for his crimes.

He confessed that he killed the children, but of course said the devil made him do it. He testified, "It is very true, my lords, that I have ravished children from their mothers. These children, I have killed them or had them killed, by slitting their throats with dagger or knife, or by separating the head from the body with axe, or by breaking the skull with stick or hammer, or by splitting their chest, or by opening their belly. Sometimes, by attaching them with a cord to an iron hook, other times by burning them..."

His actions were so sadistic that during his trial the justices found some of the testimony extremely disturbing and removed many passages from the official record because they were too graphic. The testimony was so obscene that pictures of Jesus and the Virgin Mary were covered to protect them from the risqué language in the court.

De Rais, Poitou, and another accomplice were hanged on October 26, 1440.

Gilles de Rais, looking bullet-proof in his armor

Evita!

Oh what a circus! Oh what a show!
Argentina has gone to town
Over the death of an actress called Eva Peron
We've all gone crazy
Mourning all day and mourning all night
Falling over ourselves to get all
Of the misery right

July 26, 1952 marks the anniversary of the death of former Argentine First Lady Eva Peron. Obviously, if your life becomes an Andrew Lloyd Weber musical, you must be an interesting person. Long before marrying Juan Peron, Evita, as she was known to her adoring followers, was an actress. Hopefully she was a more a gifted thespian than Madonna, who played her on the big screen.

Eva and Juan waving to their fans!

Eva Peron became the Argentine first lady in 1946. Putting aside the Madonna references, Peron was an amazing political force in Argentinean politics. As first lady, she leveraged her popularity to take up the issue of workers' rights; she helped the poor, pushed for women's suffrage, and even started an all-women political party, the *Feminist Peronist Party*.

In 1951, she accepted the Feminist Peronist Party's nomination to become Vice President. While she was very popular with the average citizens, the Argentine aristocracy, and military elite, she eventually dropped out of the race for health reasons. She died of cervical cancer at the age of 33.

Eva and Juan in 1945

Prior to her death, the Argentine legislature named her the Argentine National Spiritual Leader. If had not been for her poor health, this would have been heady stuff for a poor girl born out of wedlock. On the news of her death, Argentina observed two days of mourning. Plans were made to construct a shrine that would have been larger than the Statute of Liberty, with Eva's body to be on display at the base of the statute.

It took nearly two years for the shrine to be built. Meantime, Juan Peron's government was deposed in a successful military coup, and he had to jet out of town in the middle of the night. Before leaving, Juan Peron did not have time to secure Eva's body. The military regime removed Eva's body from display and made it a crime to mention of the name Peron. The whereabouts of her body were unknown for 16 years until finally the dictatorship revealed that she had been buried in Milan, Italy.

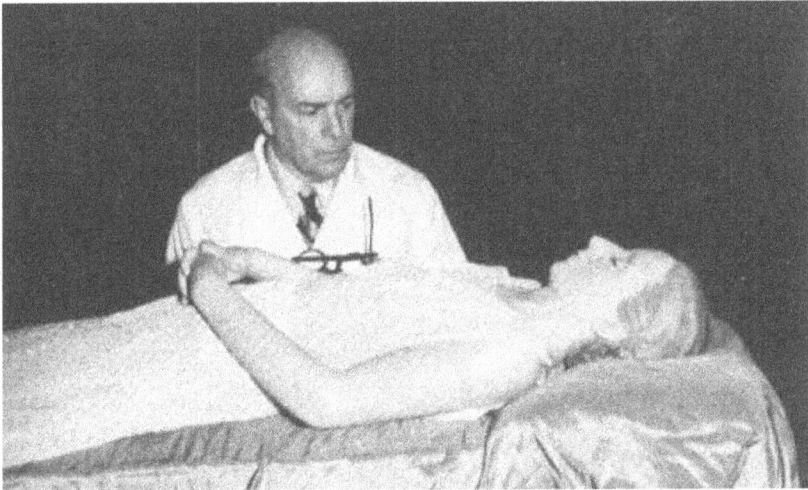

Dr. Pedro Ara inspects the embalmed body

In 1973, Juan Peron came out of exile, returned to Argentina, and was elected president again. He died in office in 1974, and his third wife Isabella, who had been elected Vice President, succeeded him. Isabella became the first female head of state in the Western Hemisphere.

Most Missingest Man in America

I find it very curious about what would motivate someone to walk away from their life without a trace. The idea of staging one's death or disappearance is intriguing, and fills our literature and movie theatres. One such case caught my eye way back when I was a senior in high school, that being the Judge Crater disappearance.

Joseph F. Crater disappeared without a trace

On August 6, 1930, Joseph F. Crater went missing. He was tall, dapper, and an associate Justice on the New York Supreme Court. He was active in the New York social scene. On the evening of his disappearance, he had dinner with friends and then caught a cab to a Broadway show where he had previously purchased theatre tickets. He was last seen wearing a brown double-breasted pin stripped suit with white spats.

It is no secret that Crater was connected to the infamous Tammany Hall. After graduating from Columbia Law School in 1913, he hung out his law shingle and almost immediately got involved in politics. He became president of the Democratic Club of Manhattan, which was closely tied to Tammany, and his legal practice grew rapidly making Crater a wealthy man. In April 1930, he withdrew $20,000, which was the standard Tammany payoff for a political appointment. A few days later, he was appointed to the Supreme Court.

Of course, the investigators looking into his disappearance learned that the 20 grand proved to be a wise investment. In the few short months after being elected to the Supreme Court, Crater was assigned to oversee a bankruptcy case. It was his duty to liquidate assets of a bankrupt hotel property. He snatched up the property himself for $75,000. Two months later, the City of New York bought the property for $3 million for a street widening project. Nice profit!

In 1916, Crater married Stella Wheeler, a wealthy woman whose divorce Crater had handled the previous year. Witnesses and associates reported that the Crater marriage was happy, although the judge also was reported to have a healthy appetite for showgirls. In July 1930, Crater and Stella were on vacation in Maine. Mrs. Crater said he received a call, and while she did not hear the conversation he later said he had to go back to the city to 'straighten those fellows out.' He left his wife and instead of dealing with his business in New York, witnesses saw him in Atlantic City with a showgirl.

Mrs. Stella Crater searches for missing husband

On August 3, 1930, he was back at his office, and his assistant reported he worked private behind closed doors for three days. On the morning of August 6, 1930, the day he went missing, he and his assistant Joseph Mara worked for about two hours cleaning out files in his office. He sent Mara to cash two checks that totaled $5,150 and then they carried two locked brief cases to Crater's apartment. He let Mara have the rest of the day off.

International manhunt begins!

Later in the day on August 6th, Crater went to a Broadway ticket office and bought a single ticket to a comedy at the Belasco Theatre called the *Dancing Partners*. He had seen the play before but liked the girls in the show. He went to a steak house for dinner and ran into some fellow lawyers with their professional dates. His friends noted that he was in a good mood showing no signs he was planning his own disappearance. He left his friends around 9 p.m. and caught a cab.

That was the last time anyone saw Joseph F. Crater.

What is odd about the story is that initially no one missed him. His wife called friends in New York ten days later when he did not return to Maine. On August 25th, he failed to show up for the opening day of the court session. Instead of calling the police, his fellow justices did a private investigation to try to find him. No one freaked out when he went missing for a few weeks. Perhaps Crater had a personal history of going off on his own for extended periods.

On September 3, 1930, almost a month after he disappeared, the police were finally notified. The story made the front page of ever newspaper in the country. Despite the publicity of the case, the investigation quickly came to a standstill. His safe deposit box had been cleaned out and the two briefcases his assistant had helped carry to the apartment were never recovered. Since the Crater case garnered so much media attention, the police were diverted into chasing countless false leads and presumed sightings of the missing jurist, which never panned out.

Everyone wanted to know if the Judge had disappeared on his own or whether his Tammany associates had killed him. A Grand Jury was called to interview witnesses: They heard from 95 witnesses and collected nearly 1000 pages of testimony. At the end of the day, they had no better idea of the whereabouts of Judge Crater than they did when the story broke.

Mrs. Crater continued to insist that her husband was a crime victim, and her conviction grew stronger when a few months later she discovered that Joe hid a life insurance policy, several uncashed checks, and a cryptic note that outlined his financial holdings. In 1937, she sued the insurance companies to pay double indemnity on the policies since he had been murdered. Her attorney floated the theory that the $5,150 was hush money Crater paid a call girl whom blackmailed him. When she demanded more and he refused, one of her gangster friends showed up to scare the judge. The lawyer speculated Judge Crater might have been accidently killed. The jury did not buy the theory and denied Mrs. Crater's double indemnity plea.

In 1939, Judge Crater was officially declared dead but reports of his sightings continued through the 1950s. In addition to the sightings, many theories emerged about what happened to him. Some posit that Crater was killed before he could testify against his Tammany Hall keepers. Other theories circulated that he was with a prostitute, accidently died, and his body was disposed of by some criminal element. Still others insist that he simply disappeared and started a new life in some exotic location.

In 2005, the case took an interesting turn when a 91-year-old Queens's widow died and left a box of notes about the case in her basement. She wrote that her husband heard the story from the cab driver who picked up Judge Crater that night in front of the steak house. The cabbie drove a couple of blocks where he picked up a couple more men and they all drove to Coney Island where the Judge was killed and buried under the Coney Island Bridge.

The area had been excavated in the 1950s, but police were not able to connect this story with any missing bodies recovered in the area over the years. Author Richard Tofel said he heard the widow's story, but was never able to find witnesses that actually saw Crater get into a cab. Tofel speculated that Crater was known to be fond of several of the chorus girls in the play that he had tickets to see. Tofel speculates that Crater most likely caught the second act of the show, and believes that Crater died in the arms of a prostitute in a brothel and Tammany Hall covered up the story.

What ever happened, it was a great story!

Sex Scandals in South Carolina

Who could forget the salacious sex scandal of South Carolina governor Mark Sanford in the summer of 2009? Of course, Mr. Sanford is certainly not the first governor or politician, for that matter, to find himself in this sort of pickle. He is not even the first South Carolina politician to have a sex scandal. When I heard of Sanford's affair with his Argentine hottie, I thought oh heck that's nothing compared to James Hammond's sex scandal in 1836.

This would be a good time to start keeping score, kids, because our friends at Wikipedia got this one wrong. Wikipedia noted that Hammond was elected to the House of Representatives in 1835 and served one year, only to give up his seat due to health reasons.

The Wikipedia knuckleheads note that he spent the next two years in Europe recovering from his illness, but the real story is not so neat and tidy... Oh yes, Mr. Hammond was recovering all right! He was recovering from his brother-in-law's threats to blackmail him. It turns out that Congressman Hammond had seduced his underage nieces, and their papa was not any too happy with the news.

Even in antebellum South Carolina, child molestation was frowned upon. Yet, Hammond did return to politics after his blackmail-induced political sabbatical. He eventually served the Palmetto State as governor and senator. The Wiki folks do note that he fathered a child with one of his slaves. Given the time, this is not particularly scandalous since most slaveholders also kept slave mistresses.

Since child molestation only derailed his political career for a few years, it is a good thing the news of his college affair with a male classmate never surfaced. Historian Martin

Duberman discovered that Mr. Hammond had engaged in, *oh my gosh*, a homosexual affair in the 1820s.

James Hammond, the writhing bedfellow of Jeffrey Winters

Perhaps even more noteworthy he was able to carry out that affair deep in the heart of Dixie. He did not even need to travel to the Minneapolis Airport to do the deal like modern day politicians looking for some hot man-on-man action.

Now I need to keep this G-rated since I hope my mom will read this book, so I am going to spare you all the juicy details of the explicit language in the letters. However, deep in the soft underbelly (pun is intended) of the South Carolina Historical Society rest the love letters written to young James by his classmate Jeffrey Winters and self-described 'writhing bedfellow'.

Mr. Winters did not rise to the same political heights as his soon to be famous lover, but he did become a Circuit Court of Appeals Judge. The affair happened when both young men were college students at what is now the University of South Carolina—GO GAMECOCKS!

Black Bart

Americans are certainly fascinated with robbers. The successful scores of these armed bandits seem like the ultimate 'get rich quick' schemes. We like to immortalize robbers as if they were folk heroes. Their lives on the run seem romantic and their instant riches seem glamorous. Their stories resemble modern day Robin Hood tales, sticking it to the rich.

Charles E. Boles aka 'Black Bart'

Don't we all fantasize about what it would feel like to stick it to the man just once in our lives? We often forget, though, that most robbers enter into criminal careers after some horrific event that left them with no other choice but to take desperate measures.

Most robbers are violent and their criminal careers end in ferocious showdowns. Innocents often become collateral damage in the execution of their crimes. One notable exception to the brutality and savage characteristics of the average highwayman was Charles Boles, also known as Black Bart.

Black Bart's criminal career lasted between 1875 and 1883, and his favorite targets involved holding up Wells Fargo Stagecoaches. For what they charged me in student loan interest, I can hardly fault Bart for his crimes against the future mega bank.

While Black Bart certainly was not the only person holding up stagecoaches in the 1870s, what set him apart was his approach to the crime. Black Bart never fired a weapon, in any of his robberies. He was always on foot, and always took a gentle if not a polite tone with his victims. Some accounts even note that in the majority of robberies his rifle was unloaded. He made a point of never robbing the stage passengers or crew of their personal belongings.

In total, Black Bart completed 28 successful stage robberies and was eventually wounded on his 29th attempt. The injury led to his capture and arrest, and he was convicted and sentenced to six years in San Quentin Prison. He was released after four years for good behavior and tried to make it in San Francisco, but the Wells Fargo detectives followed him everywhere he went. He eventually was able to give them the slip and seemed to vanish off the face of the Earth, never to be seen again.

Lift your Glass to Sam

In addition to having his name adorn a popular beer, Sam Adams was a most intriguing guy, a true American story and a leading organizer of the American Revolution. The son of a wealthy Boston merchant, Sam Adams (Junior) was a mess like many sons of successful men. Adams failed to finish his law studies, burned through his inheritance, botched his job as a tax collector, and ran the family brewery into the ground. The beer that carries his name is a 20th century creation and was unveiled in 1985 by the Boston Brewing Company.

Sam Adams: ne'er-do-well, inept business owner, failed brew master, and revolutionary rock star

It was a good thing for the American revolutionary cause that Adams did not have business acumen. After running the family brewery out of business he was able to concentrate his new found free time on working the Boston crowds into a rebellious furry. What he lacked as a capitalist he more than made up for as a revolutionary.

Adams was instrumental in organizing Bostonians to stand united against the 1764 Sugar and 1765 Stamps Acts. His growing popularity and charisma earned him a seat in the Massachusetts Legislature in 1765, and he quickly positioned himself in a leadership position in that assembly. Following the 1770 Boston Massacre where British soldiers were spooked into firing into a rowdy crowd of protesters, Sam Adams found he had a knack for political organizing. Adams began corresponding with the revolutionaries in other colonies in order to ensure the citizens of the Thirteen British Colonies would stand united against what Adams deemed as aggressive and punitive actions by the British government.

Many also consider Adams to be the architect of the Boston Tea Party, and after the British closed the Boston Harbor in 1774 he became more radicalized and aggressive in his revolutionary rhetoric. Even while conservative colonists were advocating for reconciliation Adams continued to push for revolution.

Adams was not above revolting from his own family views either. When his cousin John was president, he aligned himself with the political followers of Thomas Jefferson his cousin's chief rival.

So if you have become dissatisfied with going with the flow and want to shake things up, go ahead lift your glass to Sam Adams and be a revolutionary.

Oy Vey! The Red Coats Are Coming!

I am sure we all remember the Longfellow poem that begins:

LISTEN, MY CHILDREN, AND YOU SHALL HEAR
OF THE MIDNIGHT RIDE OF PAUL REVERE...

Paul Revere rides like a wild man through the Boston suburbs

Way back in the day, we learned this little ditty in grade school. Some may have also learned that there is a darker side to this story and one that may have an anti-Semitic slant. Since we know Americans like to create folk heroes and can be racist, it is certainly easy to assume the Paul Revere story might be too good to be true.

True enough, Revere was an express messenger rider and was sent on April 18, 1775 to ride from Boston to Lexington to warn Sam Adams and John Hancock that the British soldiers were marching out to arrest them. He hung out his lanterns in the prearranged signal in the event he was not allowed to leave the city. Revere did make the famous ride and successfully alerted the Massachusetts countryside of the British march to arrest colonist militiamen.

His 17-mile journey was immortalized in the Longfellow poem, and as a result he became an American folk hero. Legend suggests that the real hero of the story was a young Jewish rider that made the 345-mile trip from Boston to Philadelphia to inform the Continental Congress of what had happened at Lexington and Concord.

That man was Israel Bissell, and the lore is that it took him five days to make the journey. Some speculate that we hear little of Bissell's ride due to anti-Semitism. For those of you keeping score at home, this is another one that our colleagues at Wikipedia got wrong. While it would be cool to imagine that this ride actually happened, no historical record has been found to substantiate this claim.

We first need to examine the facts to determine if there was even a chance the story could happen as has been retold. First, the average express rider was able to trot along on the crappy colonial roads at the rate of around 2–4 miles an hour. I know that seems slow, but the roads were horrible and he had to stop in each town so the local scribes could hand-copy the message. This would have slowed the rider down even more. The only way Bissell could have made the ride is if he had ridden pretty much non-stop, never slept and constantly replaced his horses along the way. It is possible, but highly unlikely, that one person could have sat in the saddle for that long. More importantly, it was not what he was ordered to do—but more about that in a second.

We know that it was customary for the courier to stop along the way and for the message to be copied so it could appear in newspapers and handbills. While it was customary for the courier's actual name to be included with the message, this was not always the reality. Sometimes in the haste to hand-copy important or timely messages, the exact name or spelling of the courier would not have been made.

Even though the name Bissell did make it all the way to Philadelphia, there is no historical record to prove that Bissell actually delivered the message. In fact, there were similar copies of this message that made it as far south as Charleston and Williamsburg with Bissell's name still attached. It is highly unlikely that Bissell would have been sent on such a long journey and further proof that the story was so hot that in the heat of the moment the scribe simply forgot to update the message with the right courier's name.

Additionally there were several versions and spellings of the name transcribed between Massachusetts and Philadelphia. This further ads to the mystery and lends credence that many riders carried the message to Philadelphia. We also know that on the morning of April 19, 1775 the post rider in Watertown, CT was charged with alerting the Connecticut countryside.

One of the regular post riders was a guy named Isaac Bissell, not Israel Bissell, and the record appears that Isaac spent almost a week riding around the colony doing his job. In the summer of 1775, Isaac Bissell petitioned payment for his expenses for the six days of work for what he called his ride "to Hartford."

If Isaac Bissell had gone all the way to Philadelphia, wouldn't he have asked to be paid for the trip? If it had taken him 5–6 days to ride down there, it should have taken him at least that long to ride back. So why did Isaac Bissell only ask for 6 days of expenses? It seems very likely that this Isaac Bissell fellow never left Connecticut.

What about the argument that there could have been two riders named Bissell? Good in theory, but the story has one small problem.

There is no historical record of any person named Israel Bissell in the colonies at this time. There are no birth or death records and certainly no payment history for what would have been his historic ride. No official accounts at the time specifically note that anyone named Bissell was in Philadelphia. It was just a spelling error, not anti-Semitism. We have not yet heard confirmation on Longfellow's position on the matter.

A Revolutionary Pain in the Neck

July 28, 1794 marks the anniversary of the death of French revolutionary Maximilien Robespierre. During the French Revolution, Big Max ran a group called the Committee of Safety, which was a cool thing to be in charge of since it gave him political license to condemn all his enemies to death.

Is it just me or do the images of French Revolution mass executions have a carnival vibe to them?

The main target of the French Revolution's blood bath was the king and queen, as well as most of the French aristocracy. Robespierre condemned King Louis XVI and Queen Marie Antoinette to death. Of course, the main downfall of French revolutionaries was that they began to turn on each other. In very short order, Robespierre lost political power and popularity, and, as the Buddhists would say, was able to realize his karma in his lifetime when he was also executed. In honor of Robespierre's death, *Killer History* brings a discussion of the French Revolution's execution method of choice: May we present Mme. Guillotine?

At its basic level, the guillotine was a grizzly device used to separate an individual from his or her head. Usually, large crowds would form to watch the public decapitations, and in the case of the French Revolution became quite vocal in their calls for the aristocrat's blood to be spilt. The execution itself took a split second to happen, with gravity doing the work to drop the giant blade across the condemned individual's neck, thus severing the head from the body.

The guillotine was not the first mechanical device used for decapitation, but found its place when the French revolutionaries in their attempt to create rules of governance took up the issue of executions in its newly established penal code. Dr. Guillotine, obviously with an angle for self-promotion of his invention introduced rules to the assembly that mandated executions should be via decapitation. He suggested that the assembly adopt the device that he had designed and offered a series of sketches of the new death machine in the fall of 1789. That's right kids, Guillotine was a medical doctor, but obviously, he forgot his Hippocratic Oath.

While the assembly initially mocked the good doctor's death machine, they did adopt his other penal code suggestions, which included the standardization of punishments on a national level, the treatment of the accused/condemned individual's family, the prohibition against the seizure of the accused/condemned individual and/or their family's property, and the safe return of the executed person's body after death.

It took a couple of years of debate before the assembly could agree to retain execution and then further discussion on finding a humane method. Most of the members of the assembly felt that previous execution methods were just too brutal for a modern society. Eventually, support for decapitation started to grow since it was such a quick and accurate method to put someone to death, and consequently the adoption of Dr. Guillotine's killing machine found its grove in 1791. You read that right kids, the French thought decapitation was a more humane way to execute someone.

Dr. G. really stuck his neck out for French penal reforms

The first decapitation machine was built and tested on corpses. After a few tweaks were made, a final version was ready for prime time. The first Guillotine execution happened in the spring of 1792.

One of the not so significant impacts of the Guillotine was it leveled the playing field for executions. Before this device was built, only the rich and infamous were decapitated in France, and throughout Europe for that matter. The Guillotine enabled even the most common criminal to be humanely executed.

By the end of 1799, nearly 15,000 people had been executed in France, including many of the members of the Assembly that had called for its implementation. It is indeed ironic that so many of the machine's early champions lost their head over its adoption.

The French last deployed the Guillotine in 1977 when they executed Hamida Djandoubi. In 1981, they abolished the death penalty.

Hitler's Bloodless Coup

On August 2, 1934, Adolph Hitler became the Supreme Commander of Germany. Since we often think of Hitler in terms of executing the Final Solution against European Jews and invading his neighbors, I find my students are often surprised to learn that Hitler came to power through a bloodless revolution and a loophole in the German Constitution.

Young Adolph sporting a nifty 'stache

Hitler was never elected to his position of German Chancellor, but was appointed by the beloved and ancient President Paul von Hindenburg, who died on August 2, 1934 at the age of 87. Upon learning of the death of the much-admired von Hindenburg, Hitler made an announcement, which stated the German government's intention to combine the positions of Chancellor and President into one position.

Paul von Hindenburg had intended upon his death for Germany to revert into monarchy. Hitler just ignored the old man's wishes, and forced German military officers to swear their allegiance to him and his government.

President Paul von Hindenburg with his own nifty 'stache

This oath became known as the Hitler Oath, and every German military officer solemnly swore, "I swear by God this sacred oath that to the leader of the German empire and people, Adolf Hitler, supreme commander of the armed forces, I shall render unconditional obedience and that as a brave soldier I shall at all times be prepared to give my life for this oath." A vote by the German people was scheduled on August 19, 1933 to legitimize his government.

An intense publicity campaign in support of Hitler's leadership was conducted in the German press. The net result was 90% of German voters endorsed Hitler serving in the combined role of Chancellor and President. Nearly all of the registered voters turned out to the polls giving Hitler an unbelievable mandate. Let me be specific here, 95% of the registered voters showed up at the polls with 90% voting for Hitler. Does anyone else smell something funny about these numbers?

Hitler and von Hindenburg

On August 20, 1934, Hitler required all Germans to sign loyalty pledges to his government. In these pledges, Germans vowed their support to Hitler, not to the German state, or to the German Constitution. Once his government was legitimized, he had the military in his control and the people under his thumb. Hitler was able to begin his march toward becoming one of the most infamous world leaders of all time.

Bataan Death March

When I was in Korea in the mid-1980s, I had the opportunity to visit Inchon. The town is beautiful—other than the giant statue of General Douglas MacArthur overlooking the harbor. There was something about that statue that rubbed me the wrong way.

I looked up the giant phallic representation of the 'great' general and thought he looked like a tool. After learning more about MacArthur's military career and specifically that he abandoned over 70,000 Americans in the Philippines in early 1942, I came to appreciate the salty language President Truman used after relieving the General of his duties. Truman said, "I DIDN'T FIRE HIM BECAUSE HE WAS A DUMB SON-OF-A-BITCH, ALTHOUGH HE WAS."

General Douglas MacArthur wets his pants on the US re-taking the Philippines

The United States had maintained a military presence in the Philippines since the 1890s following the Spanish–American War. The island nation had been an important naval port to support US commercial vessels transporting the haul of made-in-America products being shipped to Asia (yeah I know it sounds funny, but once upon a time the United States actually produced things). At the start of WWII, the US military had a combined US/Filipino force of 75,000 men stationed in the Philippines.

After successfully executing the attack on Pearl Harbor, the Japanese military turned its attention to other American holdings in the Pacific. When it looked like the Japanese were going to attack the Philippines, MacArthur left his soldiers and made the quote he is famously known for: "I'LL BE BACK!"

The Japanese quickly stormed through the Philippines, and the US forces retreated to the easily defended Bataan Peninsula to hunker down and wait for MacArthur to send support. As the early months of 1942 slipped by, the support never showed up. The US troops in Bataan were not resupplied, although it would have been difficult to get supplies through the Japanese blockade. There is little evidence that MacArthur even tried to get the US forces off the Philippines.

As January slipped into February, the soldiers went down to half rations, and as March approached they went down to ¼ rations. Unknown to the Japanese commanders when they staged their assault in early April 1942, the US forces had not eaten in several days. Although there were about ten times as many Americans as the Japanese were prepared to handle, the fight was fast and furious, and the Japanese military quickly captured the US force in Bataan.

US troops surrender on the Bataan Peninsula

This was the largest American-led military force ever to surrender. As such, the real problem for the Japanese then began: What to do with this many captives? The plan was to march the POWs to put them on a train and then to ship them to POW camps in Japan. The march to the train was longer than anticipated and about 10,000 Americans died on the forced march of 55 miles following the surrender.

The Americans were much weaker than the Japanese expected; those that could not keep up were bayoneted in the sweltering Filipino sun. While over 50,000 soldiers made it to the POW camps, the conditions they were held in were even more despicable. Only a couple thousand of the Bataan soldiers survived to the end of the war.

The US Marines proclaim they will never leave a buddy behind, and this may be at the crux of MacArthur's problem—he was not a Marine.

What Were They Thinking?

The crew of the Enola Gay looking well... Evidently, they liked their short shorts.

On August 9, 1945, a second nuclear bomb was dropped on the Japanese city of Nagasaki, killing 80,000 people. The bomb dropped three days earlier on Hiroshima, killed 140,000. By the summer of 1945, the US most certainly had the upper hand in WWII's Pacific theater. The fight was not easy; it was a grinding, brutal blood bath, but the momentum was leaning strongly towards the United States.

First atomic explosion over Hiroshima, Japan
August 6, 1945

The Japanese War Council, or the gang that could not make up their minds

There was no way out for Japan, and the US was poised to launch a ground invasion of the Japanese mainland. The only thing standing in the way between this US invasion and what would surely be the total destruction of this culture was the agreement by the Japanese War Council to throw in the towel and accept an unconditional surrender. The civilian representatives wanted to raise the white surrender flag, but the military was resolute in its desire to maintain its Samurai honor and they refused to quit. The War Council was at a stalemate when the US bombed Hiroshima.

It is so easy to look at this devastating event and say, sure, if I was in that position I would hold up my hands and shout as loudly as possible, "I've had enough!" This sort of reaction seems logical when faced with the most destructive bomb ever built just unleashed on your country and you have no way of fighting back against it. Oh heck yeah, I'm throwing in the towel.

Yet that is not what happened on August 7, 8, and 9, 1945. The United States anxiously waited for the message of the Japanese surrender to filter its way through diplomatic channels. But the message never came.

So the question should be what on earth was going through the heads of the Japanese War Council that prevented them from surrendering? Did they think they could fight their way back? Did they think this was just the motivational tool that they could leverage to call the Japanese civilians to retaliate against the Americans?

Did they think the US was a one-shot wonder and did not have the resources to fire off another nuclear bomb? Were they banking on the Soviets entering the fight and helping to broker a better deal?

Historians have argued all sides of this case and make compelling arguments. One camp notes the dropping of the bombs saved lives. Revisionist historians argue that the use of the atomic bombs came as an early Cold War show of force for the Soviets and an attempt to end the war early in order keep Stalin out of the fight. Japanese-American Historian Tsuyoshi Hasegawa argues that the Japanese leaders knew the war was over and they were losing. Nevertheless, in Japanese culture these two issues—defeat and surrender do not necessarily co-exist as they do in the west. Surrendering is a political act and the Japanese did not have a history of surrendering.

The military wanted to maintain their honor and the honor of the Emperor while the civilians wanted to make a deal. The War Council needed a unanimous decision in order to act—and in early August, they were at a stalemate. The Council needed something huge to happen in order to save their honor. The dropping of the two nuclear bombs and Stalin's declaration of war on August 8th provided just the right political cover. Recently declassified documents in Japan support this notion. Mitsumasa Yonai, a War Council Member and the Japanese Naval Minister, described the bombs as a *"gift from heaven."* Without the bombs, the Japanese military was preparing for the US invasion of mainland Japan in the fall of 1945.

Fortunately, that invasion did not have to happen. The Japanese did surrender following the August 9 bombing of Nagasaki, Stalin was kept out of the fight, and US companies were allowed to profit from the rebuilding of the Japanese economy.

US troops celebrate the end of World War II

Ike's Dykes

World War II brought many changes to modern warfare. Most notable of those changes was the high number of women that served in uniform. The Women's Army Corp, or WAC as it was commonly known, had over 150,000 female soldiers. These female warriors served in vital support roles, which enabled the Army to function at a high level.

General Eisenhower looking pretty butch

General Dwight D. Eisenhower's European command utilized a WAC battalion of over 900 women to perform logistical and clerical duties that assisted in the rebuilding of the continent following the war. Since this was way before Don't Ask Don't Tell legislation, the Army routinely dismissed gay and lesbian soldiers merely on the hint of their presumed illicit sexuality.

The LGBT legend insists that these early WAC battalions contained a significantly high number of lesbians. Eisenhower's own staff was not immune to these stereotypes. Reacting to observations, rumors, and complaints from fellow officers, Ike decided to clean house. He ordered a WAC NCO, Sergeant Johnnie Phelps, to prepare a list of all the lesbians in his command so they could be promptly discharged.

Phelps estimated that around 95% of the WAC soldiers in Eisenhower's headquarters command were indeed lesbian. Sergeant Phelps agreed to make the list, but she also reminded Ike that this WAC battalion was one of the most decorated, had the least disciplinary problems, the fewest incidents of venereal diseases, lowest pregnancy rates (they were lesbians after all), and fewest unexcused absences of any WAC unit in the Army. Dismissing these valued soldiers would have a significant impact on accomplishing their mission.

Ike shook his head, but said he wanted the list anyway. Sergeant Phelps then told her commanding officer that she would abide by his order, but he needed to know something about the list. In her thick Carolina accent, Sergeant Phelps said, "I'll make your list, but you've got to know that when you get the list back, my name's going to be first."

Eisenhower withdrew the order. Following the war, Johnnie Phelps became an activist and leader in the women's movement and headed up the Los Angeles chapter of NOW.

WWII WACs throw their hats in the air!

The Living Unknown Soldier

I have always found cases of amnesia fascinating and frightening. The thought of losing one's memory and not being able to recall any aspect of your past must be terribly disconcerting for the person suffering from the rare memory malady. When I heard about the WWII case of Charles A. Jameson, I was not only intrigued, but also felt empathy for his plight. The Jameson case was, as historian William Breuer noted, the only known living Unknown Soldier.

In early February 1945, military transport ship the USS LeJeune arrived in Boston with a load of wounded sailors, marines, and soldiers. One injured combatant was badly wounded, his back full of shrapnel, and he had a major head injury. His only identification was a tag tied to his body: "Charles A. Jameson, 49, Catholic; citizenship, American, *Cutty Sark.*"

Since the man known as Jameson was in a coma and it would take nearly three years for his wounds fully to heal, it would be a while for the hospital staff to fully recognize the extent to which they had a mystery man on their ward. The Red Cross and the US military tried in vain to identify Jameson in order to notify his family. The US Coast Guard, US Navy, and the Merchant Marine had no record of the patient.

Since the tag on Jameson when he arrived at the hospital stated that he was aboard the Cutty Sark, a search for the crew records were conducted. It was discovered that the Cutty Sark had sunk 100 years earlier.

His image was published widely in the United States and in Europe, but no one ever stepped forward to identify him.

Eventually Jameson regained consciousness and due to his deafness was only able to communicate by writing on a pad. In detail, he described the Royal Gunnery School in Gosport, England. The search for Jameson's identity turned to the British Maritime Registry, but that also turned out to be a dead end—the British had no records for a Charles A. Jameson.

One day, he wrote that he thought he had been the First Mate on a merchant ship the *Hinemoa* and that it had sunk in the Atlantic. The *Hinemoa* was actually sunk in the English Channel, not in the Atlantic. Further confounding investigators, survivors of the *Hinemoa* were shown a picture of Jameson and no one could identity him.

The man named Charles A. Jameson lived his remaining 12 years at the hospital without a single visitor and never knowing his own identity.

Sugar Momma of the Country

I was relating to my class how George Washington came to marry the slightly older, but fabulously wealthy, Martha Dandridge Custis when one of my students interrupted and stated what seemed to be the obvious—George Washington had gotten himself a sugar momma. I had to laugh because while I had not considered it that way, when you look at the facts it does appear that Big George might have married Martha for her money.

Matronly Martha Washington

Martha was after all slightly older than George and the wealthiest widow in the Virginia colony. At a not so close inspection of her first lady portrait, it is pretty obvious that she reminds me much more of Barbara Bush than Jackie Kennedy.

We know from historical record that Washington was obsessively ambitious, and well heck, he would not be the first to marry for money, even in Colonial Virginia.

With that in mind, I was quite surprised to discover that Martha's first husband Daniel Custis was nearly written out of his father's will for considering Martha as his bride. Daniel was about 20 years older than Martha, and his father was one of the wealthiest planters in Virginia. With that much bank, it would seem that Daniel Custis could have his pick of any of the lovely ladies of Virginia, but he was willing to brave poverty in order to marry 15-year-old Martha. Old Man Custis had already vetoed several potential brides, saying they were beneath this son's station and he thought Martha Dandridge was a gold digger.

Daniel's dad meant business, and to prove his point he gave away big parts of the estate to two of his mistresses. Daniel held his ground, and eventually the old man relented and gave Daniel the remaining part of the estate on the condition he and Martha raised Daniel's half-brother until he reached the age of majority and could control his inheritance.

Now here is the catch: The half-brother was called Mulatto Jack, and yes, was the product of father Custis's relationship with one of his slaves. The old man had to know this would cause some strain on the newlyweds' relationship.

The marriage between Daniel and Martha lasted about ten years and produced two children that survived to adulthood. Upon Daniel Custis's death, Martha was 26 and the wealthiest widow in the colony. She had 1700 acres, 300 slaves and a line of potential suitors a country mile long. Washington was tall, handsome, from a good family, and not so coincidently flat out broke. Despite his lack of financial prospects, the young George Washington was a military superstar serving as the colonel of the Virginia militia during the Seven Years' War.

Since Martha destroyed their correspondence upon George's death, we do not know for sure what they saw in each other. Historians have speculated that she saw the potential of the 25-year-old Washington. Certainly, the ambitious future father of our country realized the potential that Martha's cash could do for his career. But I still can't get the vision of the double-chinned First Lady portrait out of my head.

However, recent scholarship has made me recalculate my perspective. Age regression techniques similar to those used on *America's Most Wanted* were applied to a Martha Washington portrait to reveal what she would have looked like at 26 when she and George hooked up. It turns out that Martha was actually good looking—well I guess she would have to be if her first husband was willing to be disinherited. So not only did George Washington marry for money, but Martha was a head turner to boot—bravo George, well played!

George Washington, looking dashing with his trusty white horse

Young Martha, but does this image really do her justice?

The Gospel According to TJ

Thomas Jefferson, biblical editor

The Judeo-Christian tradition in the United States notes the ardent faithfulness of the American founding fathers. However, their level of religious engagement looks a lot different from the current images of American politicians who try to compete to determine who is the most religious. Many of the founding fathers practiced Deism, including George Washington and they believed that while a supreme being created the universe, they pretty much did not buy into all the supernatural stuff that Christianity offered. The founding fathers preferred to believe that logic and proper morals were the way go.

The religious views of Thomas Jefferson present a paradox for fundamentalists about how the founding fathers are represented. On the one hand, it is important to note the faithful wordings included in the founding documents of the American government, but questions of Jefferson's religious beliefs are and were a problem even in his time. In his 1800 presidential campaign, he had to defend his religious beliefs when he was accused of being an atheist. There are no accounts of how voters felt or if they even knew that the commander-in-chief spent his free time editing the Bible.

Of his own religious beliefs, Jefferson wrote:

> We must reduce our volume to the simple evangelists, select, even from them, the very words only of Jesus, paring off the amphibologisms into which they have been led, by forgetting often, or not understanding, what had fallen from him, by giving their own misconceptions as his dicta, and expressing unintelligibly for others, what they had not understood themselves. There will be found remaining the most sublime and benevolent code of morals which has ever been offered to man. I have performed this operation for my own use, by cutting verse by verse out of the printed book, and arranging the matter which is evidently his, and which is as easily distinguishable as diamonds in a dunghill.

Even with this admission, Jefferson's beliefs were untraditional even by 18th century standards. Other comments he made about Christianity and his revision of the Bible would surely have prevented him from getting through the Iowa primary in a modern presidential bid. He seemed obsessed with correcting the image of how the Bible depicted the life of Jesus.

The problem with the Bible, Jefferson argued, was that it covered up the message of Jesus with the 'dung of Christianity'. He set out to cut out the miracles and false information, and only presented the teachings that Jesus gave in the bible. Of his editing work Jefferson wrote to John Adams, "I have performed the operation for my own use by cutting verse by verse out of the printed book, and arranging the matter, which is evidently his and which is as easily distinguished as diamonds in a dunghill." His editing work started around 1803, right before he sent Lewis and Clark on their road trip.

Holy smokes! Impeachment proceedings were brought up against Bill Clinton for an intern polishing his knob, so can you imagine what Newt Gingrich would have done to Jefferson for his cut and paste job on the Good Book?

Jefferson whittled the Bible down to 46 pages, called his edited manuscript *The Life and Morals of Jesus of Nazareth,* and told Adams that it was "the most sublime and benevolent code of morals which has ever been offered to man." While the thought that the President of the United States desecrated this sacred text may be difficult to understand, one needs to consider that Jefferson was looking at this book through the lens of the 'enlightenment'. He was trained to question everything. The Bible was just one more thing he was not going to take for granted. It speaks volumes of Jefferson's faith that he could drill down into the life of Jesus and find real beauty and something he could get on board with. To his friend Dr. Benjamin Rush he wrote, "To the corruption of Christianity I am indeed opposed, but not to the genuine precepts of Jesus himself."

So, what would Jesus do? Read the Jefferson Bible and find out.

"Say nothing of my religion," Jefferson once said. "It is known to myself and my God alone. Its evidence before the world is to be sought in my life; if that has been honest and dutiful to society, the religion which has regulated it cannot be a bad one."

Say AMEN!

Presidential Beat Down

Andrew Jackson, with his old hickory cane in his left hand, preparing to beat his would-be assassin

Andrew Jackson was far from bullet proof, but what we do know is he may have been the toughest SOB ever to reside in the White House. For most of his life, he carried around two bullets in his body, one lodged in his shoulder and the other just below his heart, both a result of his proclivity for dueling. His lame nickname, Old Hickory, referred to the long cane he carried with him when he was in public. Historians estimate that Jackson participated in as many as 13 duels, with many of those fights resulting in injury. He also carried around the facial scar from a beating he took from a British army officer inflicted during the Revolutionary War. The Redcoat captured Jackson and his older brother as they sniped at the British Army in South Carolina.

The Officer grabbed 14-year-old Jackson and ordered him to shine his boots. In a statement that will surely melt the heart of every American nationalist, the teenager spit on the dude's boots and told him where he could stick 'em. Young Andy took the back of the officer's sword in the head leaving a wicked facial scar. His older brother also refused to shine the brute's boots, and unfortunately was beaten so badly that he died from his wounds.

Jackson was an amazingly popular president. The people loved him because he came across as such an average Joe! However, to his political enemies he did indeed rub more than a few people the wrong way. He was a polarizing figure, strongly independent and not willing to drink the political Kool-Aid in Washington. With that said, it is no surprise that in his second term someone finally tried to take him out.

In the first presidential assassination attempt, immigrant house painter, Richard Lawrence, stalked the president in the Capital Building with two loaded pistols. As Jackson and his entourage made the rounds on Capitol Hill, slapping backs and rubbing palms with the Congressional power brokers, Lawrence emerged from behind a pillar six feet from the president, aimed his pistol at Jackson, and pulled the trigger.

At nearly pointblank range, Lawrence fired his pistol at the president's chest. Everyone seemed frozen when the gun misfired. The cap exploded, but did not fire. Jackson was still standing. Deterred for only a second, Lawrence retrieved his second pistol from his bag, took aim at Jackson's chest, and fired again. As if there was an invisible force field around Jackson, the second weapon also misfired.

Not waiting around to see if Lawrence had a third weapon in his bag of tricks the 67-year-old president rushed the young man and proceeded to give him a presidential beat down with his old hickory cane.

No one is quite sure why the pistols did not fire; they were loaded correctly and fired later. Some speculate that the open grave in the Capitol Rotunda dug out for former President Washington's body caused the space to be damp and this may have resulted in the powder not firing.

A full investigation of the foiled assassination attempt revealed that Lawrence had acted alone. Jackson was not convinced by the evidence, sure his political rivals John C. Calhoun and Henry Clay had been involved. Of both men, Jackson observed later, "I have only two regrets: I didn't shoot Henry Clay and I didn't hang John C. Calhoun."

Lawrence was found to be criminally insane and sentenced to an institution.

Will Lead the Free World for Cash

Most of the early American presidents were wealthy men. This is not to imply that personal wealth was a prerequisite for the Oval Office, however given the early challenges with the federal government it did not hurt if the office holder had a bankroll to hold them over. The obligations of the presidency often kept one away from home and prevented the proper oversight of farms and businesses. Early presidents, congressmen, and government appointees would need to hire an overseer to take care of their business obligations when they were away in Washington City taking care of the nation's business.

Musical score for the Harrison/Tyler campaign song Tippecanoe and Tyler too

This financial sacrifice in some circumstances could be quite significant and create a hardship on the office holder. In addition, the finances of the young nation were not always on a firm footing either. Sometimes the US Treasury had a hard time paying its bills, and the paychecks to the president, vice-president, as well as congressmen were not always regular.

TYLER RECEIVING THE NEWS OF HARRISON'S DEATH.

Woodcut of Tyler receiving news of Harrison's death

Since most of these early leaders were wealthy men, this irregular pay schedule was only an inconvenience. But the financial constraints of public office certainly limited who was able to lead the country. Quite simply, not everyone could take off work to run for office. The financial hardships were just too great for most would-be politicians.

A major exception to this rule was Vice President John Tyler. In 1841, Tyler became vice president to William Henry Harrison. Vice President Tyler was so strapped for cash that he could not afford to rent a room in Washington for any extended length of time. He was so insolvent that he only stayed in Washington after their inauguration just long enough to open the Senate session in order to confirm Harrison's cabinet nominees. He then hustled back to his home in Williamsburg, Virginia so he did not have to pay room and board in the capital!

Back in Virginia, he waited impatiently for the postal service to bring his paycheck. At long last, the letter arrived— with what he hoped would be his long owed back salary.

Instead of his vice presidential paycheck, though, he received word that he had gotten a promotion. The missive informed Tyler he needed to report immediately to Washington, D.C. as President William Henry Harrison had suddenly died. The Harrison administration had only been in office for about a month. Tyler still had not received his paycheck.

James Tyler became the first person to become president through succession

So here is the rub, Tyler was so cash-poor that he could not afford to travel from his home in Williamsburg, VA to Washington for his own presidential inauguration.

After much hand wringing, Tyler's friends loaned him the money, and he and his family headed to the capital just in time for his inauguration. I think we can agree that this was a safe loan since everyone knew Tyler now resided at 1600 Pennsylvania Avenue. He became the tenth president of the United States and the first ever to become president via succession. In 1841, Tyler also became the youngest person to assume the presidency at 51 years of age. Of course, eventually Theodore Roosevelt would surpass that feat becoming the youngest president at 41 and John Kennedy the youngest elected president at 42.

The Tyler administration was not very noteworthy, with the admittance of Texas to the Union being its biggest accomplishment. Tyler tended to struggle with Congress, leading former president John Quincy Adams and then a congressman to initiate impeachment proceedings, which never cleared the House.

Tyler was not reelected and retired to his home in the Virginia low country where he lived outside of politics until 1861. At the start of the Civil War, he voiced his support for state's rights and southern secession. Tyler became the only former president elected to office in the Confederacy, but died before formally taking office.

John Quincy Adams doing his best Grinch imitation failed to have Tyler impeached

As a former president, Tyler's death should have resulted in the standard state funeral and national mourning period that other presidents had received. Since he had sided with the Confederacy, he was the only former president not to receive a state funeral.

Tyler also had the distinction of being the oldest former president to father a child at 70 years of age.

Whet your Horns on This One

Abe Lincoln demonstrating what might be his famous ringside stare down

Ask a complete stranger to name the first thing to come into their head when you say the name Abe Lincoln. Most likely, you're going to get a standard set of responses that range from tall, bearded, Civil War, freed the slaves, or Gettysburg Address. The one thing that folks will not mention is that he was a bad-ass wrestling champion.

The frontier wrestlers of the 19th century were starkly different from the squat young men in singlets that we may be forced to watch every four years in the Olympics. Wrestling in Lincoln's day was an all-out no holds barred affair. Make no mistake about it: this was a man's sport!

In one match, the future president disposed of his opponent in a single toss and then taunted the mob, "Any of you want to try it, come on, and whet your horns!"

Bill Green who owned a mercantile in Lincoln's adopted hometown of New Salem, Illinois observed in 1831 that the 22-year-old Lincoln could whip anybody in town. "He could out-run, out-lift, out-wrestle, and throw down any man in Sangamon County." Lincoln was tall at 6'4", but he only weighed 185 pounds. He was a beanpole! It is hard to see this side of the Great Emancipator!

Future President Abe Lincoln demonstrating one of his signature wrestling moves

Another New Salem wrestling aficionado, observed of Lincoln, "He sure was the big buck of this lick." Shortly after arriving in town, the young Lincoln gave local champion Jack Armstrong the worst beating of his life, which must have become the future president's signature victory.

Over his 12-year wrestling career, Lincoln only lost one match, in 1832. Representing his Illinois Volunteer Regiment in the Black Hawk War, he lost to Hank Thompson, who has the distinction of being the only man known to throw Lincoln in a wrestling match.

This new information about the 16th president of the United States, Abraham Lincoln, certainly helps to inform us of his character and personality. It is no wonder he was so upset during the Civil War when Union generals were reluctant to attack. Perhaps Lincoln would have had better luck convincing McClellan to go on the offensive if he had put the Union general in a presidential headlock.

Hey Big Spender!

Mary Lincoln, widow of 16th American president Abe Lincoln, is an interesting case study. Born Mary Todd to a slave holding Kentucky farmer she seemed to realize at an early age how to work the system. As a young girl, she announced that her life's ambition was to be married to the president of the United States.

Mary Lincoln sporting the fineries that ran up the mountain of debt

With this focus, her natural charm, and good looks, she passed on several upwardly mobile young men, setting her sights on the tall, clumsy unattractive Abraham Lincoln, who she described as 'brilliant'. Later in life, Mary claimed to have visions of his death so perhaps in an earlier vision she also saw his potential.

Mary Todd Lincoln was articulate, charming, and was known as an amazing hostess. Early on, she took an active role in Lincoln's political campaigns at a time when women on the campaign trail were rare. Her speaking abilities enabled her to be an effective campaign surrogate for Lincoln. Her efforts in the 1860 Presidential election certainly did more good for his eventual victory than harm.

But for all of Mary Lincoln's assets, she also posed several problems for Abe. In our 21st century lexicon, we have a word for Mrs. Lincoln's malady: She was a shopaholic. In 1861, Congress allocated $20,000 for renovations and upgrades to the White House's furnishings.

She blew through the money with such gusto that when Abe found out how much she had spent on drapes he threatened to pay for them out of his own pocket. Not only was he upset with her extravagance, he worried about how the spending would look to the citizens he was calling on to sacrifice during the nation's time of war.

Mary tried to fix the problem; she sold excess manure from the White House stable to pay some of the bills. I'm sorry, but the thought that the White House had too much manure seems just too funny to think about! Perhaps we could sell off some of the excess manure in Washington now and pay down the national debt?

Mary's high rolling ways continued, however. Evidently, she had an affinity for black evening gowns and traveled to the finest clothing sellers in New York and Philadelphia to supply her addiction. In the process, she racked up a small mountain of debt.

By the time her husband's 1864 reelection campaign came around, she was torn. She had started to have visions that he would be killed in office, but if he was reelected, she could hold off the creditors for a little while longer. If he lost the race, she would have no way of keeping the news from Abe any longer and she would have to confess her shopping addiction and her debt.

THE ASSASSINATION OF PRESIDENT LINCOLN,
AT FORD'S THEATRE WASHINGTON D.C. APRIL 14th 1865.

To complicate matters, she was also convinced that the nation needed her husband in the White House to help restore the Union.

As we know, Lincoln won in a landslide reelection and Mary's secret was safe, until John Wilkes Booth assassinated the president, that was. Then Mary Lincoln, the woman who had dedicated her life to becoming first lady was faced with a major problem. She had to leave the protection of the White House, but she did not go willingly. In fact, she barricaded herself in the upstairs bedrooms and refused to leave. It took nearly a month for Andrew Johnson to pry her out of the house. She and her two surviving sons moved to Chicago. The creditors found her, and she tried in vain to hold them off. She started selling off Abe's personal belongings as a way to pay off her debt. She sold stocks and she petitioned Congress for a pension.

Her desperation reached its apex in 1867 when she and friend Lizzie Keckly arranged to sell off some of Mary's garish gowns. They billed the sale as *Mrs. Lincoln's Second-Hand Clothing Sale* and hoped to capitalize on the public's curiosity about her husband. Virtually no one showed up to buy Mary's old clothes. Mary and Lizzie's friendship soured in 1868 when Lizzie published a tell-all story about the Lincoln marriage.

Presidential first son Robert Lincoln looking like Johnny Depp

After her third son, Tad, died in 1871, Mary's spending problems continued, as did her erratic behavior. Eventually her son Robert had her legally committed to an asylum in 1875. She spent four months at Bellevue Place, a mental hospital outside of Chicago. After her release, she lived with her sister in Springfield until her death in 1882.

First American Woman Presidential Candidate

Victoria Woodhull

The 1872 American presidential election was notable not in the victory of the extremely popular war hero U.S. Grant but in the campaign of the first woman candidate. Without a doubt, Hillary Clinton was the first viable female candidate to make a run at the nation's highest office. However, Victoria Woodhull forged the path 140 years before the former first lady narrowly lost the Democratic nomination in 2008. Ms. Woodhull failed to garner a single electoral vote, and when searching for information about the 1872 election you will barely even see a reference to her campaign. While she was certainly never a threat to the political establishment, her campaign did mark the beginning of organized protests by national organizations for women's suffrage. These protests would continue to gather support until the passage of the 19th Amendment in 1919.

Seven women attempted to vote in the 1872 election and were subsequently jailed for their protests, including Susan B. Anthony. On Election Day, candidate Woodhull was arrested for indecency. COME ON! Did they seriously think her seven voters were going to disrupt Grant's landslide victory? Hardly a recount needed!

Woodhull remains an enigma to what the typical ideal of a Victorian woman resembled. Her first step out of the social norms was the divorce from her first husband of 11 years, Dr. Channing Woodhull. By any standards the GOOD doctor was a lousy husband: He was abusive, slept around, and drank too much. Even with these transgressions against acceptable behavior, Victorian women had few social or economic freedoms, and therein is the double standard. Not only were men free to sleep around, bear no responsibility for the children produced out of wedlock, and treat their wives in pretty much any way they wished, Victorian-era men could also freely divorce their wives. Women, on the other hand, had a much harder time obtaining a divorce; while it was not impossible it was very difficult. Woodhull's successful execution of her divorce proves either that she was strong enough to fight the legal battles or that he was really a bum.

After the divorce, Ms. Woodhull entered into an emotional, physical, and business partnership with John Blood, who shared many of her ideas about social reform and belonged to a movement called Free Love. This group argued that traditional American marriages trapped people into predetermined domestic roles and limited an individual's opportunities to obtain happiness. The *free lovers*, as they were called, sought relationships that were viewed as equal partnerships. The free love advocates also noted the challenges of finding a single person that could fulfill all of an individual's needs. They supported polyamory, the ability to take multiple lovers in a non-exploitive and mutually beneficial manner. Indeed, it is noted that Ms. Woodhull had a series of lovers following her divorce and while she lived with John Blood.

It should come as little surprise that Victoria Woodhull and the free lovers were viewed as shockingly scandalous in comparison to their buttoned-down Victorian contemporaries. Ms. Woodhull thus had no chance of winning the 1872 election. With that said, I wonder what role Bill Clinton would have played in her campaign.

Grant's Black Friday

The wildly popular 18th President, U.S. Grant

The Civil War and Reconstruction years were characterized by the absence of the American two-party system in Washington. The Democrats were a Southern Party before and after the Civil War, and their absence in Washington allowed an unprecedented advancement of Republican Party policies. Most noticeably, the pro-business development programs such as support for railroad building and the Homestead Act, which serve as two examples that certainly helped western development. However, without political opposition and a healthy debate, the deregulation of American businesses during this period set the stage for several business/political scandals that nearly brought down the Grant Administration during the early 1870s. We are talking Enron, WorldCom, and Bernie Madoff all rolled into one here, folks.

Ulysses S. Grant, the victorious Union general of the Civil War, was elected president in 1868. He lived in Galena, Illinois, which was a favorite day trip when I lived in eastern Iowa. During the Civil War, Grant became quite the celebrity, and following the less than impressive presidency of Andrew Johnson, Americans hoped that Grant would work the same magic he had displayed on the battlefield in the nation's capital. But while Grant's honesty and straight-shooter personality worked well in combat, he did not always show the best personal judgment in his civilian and presidential affairs.

Economic scumbag, James Fisk

He often accepted extravagant gifts from people trying to impress and secure his help. He also allowed himself to be seen hanging out with unscrupulous business speculators such as Jay Gould and James Fisk. This association was a tad bothersome for Grant, because they were trying to corner the gold market. If they could pull this off, they would essentially control the American economy.

Gould and Fisk enlisted the help of Grant's brother-in-law Abel Corbin, who provided intelligence and manipulation of the president's actions. Corbin encouraged Grant to appoint General Daniel Butterfield as assistant secretary of the Treasury. Butterfield, who was a buddy of Gould and Fisk, was assigned the job of sounding the alarm if the government planned to release gold into the market.

In 1869, Gould and Fisk started buying and holding gold in large quantities. This drove the price through the roof.

Opportunist and swindler, Jay Gould

While Grant did eventually figure out their plans, it was not before they sent the stock market into a tailspin. Grant authorized the Treasury to flood the marketplace with gold so as to thwart their plans. On Friday September 24, 1869, also known as Black Friday, the US Treasury opened up the gold market floodgates. This flash flood of gold in the market resulted in a rapid resetting of the gold price. As the price of gold plummeted peculators were financially ruined in a matter of minutes.

Congress did investigate Grant's involvement, but was not able to prove that he was directly connected to the Gould and Fisk scheme to monopolize the gold reserves. While the scandal harmed Grant's reputation, the damage was not enough to hinder his reelection in 1872. Of course, the Grant administration would go onto bigger and more impressive scandals in his next term...

Crédit Mobilier

Cartoon depiction of the scandal-riddled Grant administration

From what we have seen in the past few pages, President Grant is more than represented on the *Presidential Scandal Walk of Shame*. He might have been much better off going back to work the family blacksmith shop in Galena, Illinois than running for president.

However, I am sure the Chamber of Commerce of the quaint little town with the plethora of antique stores in northwest Illinois would much rather promote their town as the former home of the 18th President instead of promoting that they are east of Dubuque and have a bunch of old houses. The *granddaddy* of all scandals to rock U.S. Grant's world was the *Crédit Mobilier* scandal. In fairness to Grant, this actual scandal did not begin during his watch, but heck, we can't necessarily blame Lincoln for this one since he was shot and Johnson was, well, Johnson after all.

George Train, mastermind of the great Union Pacific train swindle

This scandal involved the railroad construction company *Crédit Mobilier of America.* The joke is this company only existed on paper. It was set up by the owners of the Union Pacific Railroad Company to convince the government and the public that they had opened up the building of this important rail line to competitive bidding and *Crédit Mobilier* had won the contract. The whole scandal is somewhat hard to follow, but here goes: So, the stockholders of the Union Pacific set up this dummy corporation called *Crédit Mobilier,* which was basically a huge tax write-off. They funneled their costs and other business expenses through *Crédit Mobilier,* and as a result it made the Union Pacific Rail Road look more profitable than it really was. Of course, some of the excess business expenses included wining and dining Congressmen and government officials so they would not look very closely at the two companies' books.

One of the masterminds of this little bait switch scheme was a fellow named George Francis Train. Yeah, his name was Train and he did railroad construction, one has to love the irony. *Killer History* has yet to confirm this, but we suspect that Mr. Train reincarnated into either Ken Lay or perhaps Jeff Skilling, both of Enron shame.

Now, the gas that fueled the scam was the hype that the nation wanted to connect the two coasts by train. Evidently, the folks at Union Pacific figured this was not that difficult to do, but they convinced the government and, more importantly, the public the job was darn near impossible. In order to see this engineering 'miracle' happen Congress agreed to subsidize the construction. Union Pacific convinced Congress that they would find a company that had the engineering capacity to pull off this job and they would supervise the work. Hey presto! All change, and *Crédit Mobilier* emerged as the contract winner.

If only there were a Sarbanes Oxley audit of Union Pacific, then everything would have looked peachy! *Crédit Mobilier* would be able to submit invoices for bogus work or inflated charges to Union Pacific who would then pass on those bills to the government for reimbursement.

No one figured out that the same people owned both companies. In 1867, the head honcho at *Crédit Mobilier* offered members of Congress the opportunity to buy shares of the company at deeply discounted prices. I am not sure, but this seems fishy to me... but evidently did not to our fine elected officials who gobbled up the stock in a feeding frenzy.

The Congressmen would then turn around and sell their shares on the open market for significantly higher prices to the unsuspecting public. Of course, in gratitude for their windfall, the Congressmen would then vote to increase the appropriations spending for *Crédit Mobilier* so they could continue to build their miraculous railroad line.

The *Crédit Mobilier* stink hit the fan via some good ol' fashioned journalism during Grant's 1872 reelection campaign. The *New York Sun* broke the story that *Crédit Mobilier* had charged the government over $70 million for a project that actually only cost the company $50 million to complete. The stock prices of both *Crédit Mobilier* and Union Pacific fell in a freefall, and, of course, as we have witnessed in the recent housing market bubble, average investors hoping to get rich bought these overpriced assets and lost their shirts when the prices fell.

Congress investigated its own members that purchased discounted *Crédit Mobilier* stock, and this led to the censure of 13 Congressmen including future President James Garfield and future Vice President Schuler Colfax.

No worries, though, for the Grant Administration: Colfax was replaced on the national ticket by Henry Wilson—who was also part of the scandal. In all, 30 congressmen of both parties were found to be involved in the scandal, but even with the extent of the malfeasance the scandal did not seem to kill anyone's career. Wilson was censured, but he became Grant's running mate in the second term and Garfield would be elected to the presidency in 1880—just in time for him to become the second president to be assassinated in 1881.

Whiskey Ring

The Grant Administration was rocked with many scandals that would certainly have brought down lesser political figures. The ability of U.S. Grant to continue in light of these political distractions is a credit to his popularity.

The president's real first name was Hiram

The fact that he had just so darn many of these little ankle-biting scandals speaks volumes not only to the corruption of the Civil War and Reconstruction years but also to Grant's inability to manage effectively during his presidency.

Taxing vice has always been a popular way to pay the bills. Just as in our current political debates about increasing taxes on smoking, alcohol, and perhaps even fast food in order to pay for health care reform, the government used a tax on whiskey consumption during the 1870s in order to pay some of the bills incurred while saving the Union. While it seems like a good idea, the tax was actually eight times what it cost to produce the liquor and caused quite a crimp on business.

Orville Babcock: his name is funny enough without my additions

The large distilleries were in the Midwest, Chicago, Milwaukee, and St. Louis, and they formed an informal union that bribed government inspectors so they could purchase 'tax stickers' at a discounted price. The conspiracy was actually pretty extensive and included not only small shopkeepers but also high-ranking government officials, and cost the government several millions of dollars in tax revenue.

Secretary of the Treasury, Ben Bristow, caught wind of the scandal, and acting alone without informing the Grant administration or the attorney general in order to avoid drawing attention to his investigation he was able to break the scandal wide open in 1875. 110 individuals were convicted in the scandal and Bristow's efforts recovered $3 million in diverted funds. While Grant himself was not implicated in the scandal, his personal secretary, or what we would call today his Chief of Staff, General Orville Babcock, was indicted but not convicted due to Grant's intervention in the case.

Grant appointed a special prosecutor, John Henderson, to investigate the case, but then fired him after complaints of Grant's efforts to interfere with the investigation.

The scandals of the Grant administration characterize this political era of Republican domination as being incredibly corrupt and endemic of mismanagement and greed.

Grant's All You Can Eat

There were so many scandals during the Grant Administration that newspapers of the time referred to his presidency as the Great Barbeque because folks just helped themselves to whatever profit opportunities that might be lying around. In 1876, Secretary of War William Belknap filled his plate in what was known as the Indian Ring scandal.

US Grant Liked to be helpful to his friends

While the late 1800s is a period characterized by greed and political corruption, and if Boss Tweed is the poster boy of misplaced political trust, it was Secretary Belknap that earned the recognition as the highest-ranking political appointment to be implicated in a scandal and the first cabinet member to face impeachment.

William Belknap prior to joining ZZ Top

For all great scandals there must be opportunity, and Belknap's came via the 1870 passage of legislation that empowered the Secretary of War to appoint one or more 'trading establishments' on frontier military posts. Wow, what a license to steal!

Belknap had complete discretion to hand over these little profit centers without competitive bidding, without Congressional oversight, and without any qualifications other than how much the bidder was willing to pay under the table.

Historian George Kohn notes that Belknap's annual salary was $8,000 a year, which evidently was not enough to accommodate Mrs. Belknap in the fashion that she would like to be accustomed. The evidence is a little sketchy about who started the fraud—Mr. or Mrs. Belknap—but what is true is that the family received over $25,000 for steering only one of the many trading centers to allied partners.

Mrs. Belknap made a deal with Caleb Marsh to grant him sole control over the trading rights at Fort Sill, Oklahoma. In return for the help, Marsh sent Mrs. Belknap $12,000 annually, and after her death sent the payments directly to the Secretary.

When the other Grant scandals started to hit the fan, Congress put all offices of the administration under the microscope, and this is when Belknap's extracurricular activities became known. Newspapers called for his head and Belknap resigned his post in 1876.

Even though Belknap fell on his sword, it was not enough to appease the members of Congress who wanted to appear tough on corruption for their constituents. The House of Representatives impeached Belknap after he had resigned. During his Senate trial, his lawyers did not even address his guilt or innocence, but rather argued that impeachment was the vehicle Congress had to remove corrupt officials from office and Belknap's resignation rendered the procedure unnecessary since he was a private citizen. The tactic must have worked because the Senate was not able to reach the two-thirds majority required for conviction.

Belknap was never tried in a criminal court for his taking kickbacks; and since the bar association did not exist in the 1870s, he was allowed to continue to practice law and became a somewhat famous and successful trial lawyer in Washington, DC. Belknap died in 1890 of a heart attack and was buried with full military honors in Arlington National Cemetery, even though his involvement in the Indian Ring scandal was well known. Now, pass me the corn bread!

Grant's Tomb

So what is buried in Grant's Tomb? If you have been reading the last few pages, you will no doubt answer—dirty laundry!

Dedication of Grant's Tomb April 27, 1897

This little journey in to the life and scandals of US Grant began with a picture. My ever supportive and helpful partner Kim brought home a delightful book from one of her thrift store adventures called *The Civil War in Art*.

US Grant, stealing hearts 140 years after his death

As we were thumbing through the book, this photograph (above) of Grant caught her eye. She was immediately drawn to the image due to what she described as "Grant's confidence." Without a doubt, the image of the soldier in muddy boots oozes with machismo and bravado. I took the liberty to relay the rumors of Grant's alcoholism, which she did not seem to mind. Of course, the rumors did not matter to Lincoln either who said in response to Grant's drinking, "If it is [drink] that makes fighting men like Grant, then find out what he drinks, and send my other commanders a case."

What we can learn from the Grant administration is that being a war hero does not qualify one to be an effective president of the United States. Certainly, his war hero status enabled him to win a second term in office, but he is better known for the scandals than for his reforms. Even through all his scandals, the public continued to love and adore Grant, and there was even an attempt to nominate him to a third term in 1880. While his battlefield leadership was never questioned, his civilian judgment should certainly be placed under scrutiny.

Grant, his wife Julia, and their son Jesse

While there was never a direct link made between him and the numerous scandals, what we might assume is that either Grant was an ineffective leader or just too trusting. Even after he left office, he allowed himself to become a victim of fraud. Wall Street whiz kid Ferdinand Ward swindled Grant and other investors out of millions and then fled. The former president was left destitute and bankrupt. Around this time, he also learned he had terminal throat cancer. He forfeited his military pension when he became president and it would not be until 1958 that former presidents would receive pensions. So the guy that made a career of capitalizing on his opportunities was running out of choices.

Grant worried about the wellbeing of his wife after his death. With his incredible popularity, his story was his only marketable asset, so Grant wrote his autobiography. Mark Twain offered Grant generous royalty terms of 75% of the profits to secure the publishing rights. Grant finished the book only a few days before he died. It was an immediate financial success, netting Grant's widow nearly a half million dollars. Gertrude Stein remarked that the book was one of the finest memoirs ever written.

Who's your Daddy?

President Grover Cleveland enjoyed a sparkling reputation. He got his start in local politics in Buffalo, and served as sheriff and later as mayor. Grover's keen political skills eventually took him to the New York State governor's mansion. As governor of New York State, he earned the nickname *Grover the Good*, and it was with this reputation that he launched his presidential campaign in 1884.

Young Grover Cleveland, taken around the time he fathered Miss Halpin's son

Cleveland was a Democrat and ran for the presidency following the scandal-filled Grant administration. It looked like his path to the White House was clear sailing until the baby daddy scandal broke

The BUFFALO EVENING STANDARD first covered the story under the headline <u>A Terrible Tale</u> just two weeks before the Democratic Party was set to nominate him. Perhaps in the 21st century, Cleveland the lifelong bachelor may have faced other rumors about his personal life. Nevertheless, in the run up to the 1884 presidential nomination the newspaper broke the story that Cleveland was the father of a now 10-year-old son born out of wedlock. The love child named Oscar Cleveland resulted from Grover's longtime affair with Maria Halpin.

The first thing to come to my mind is presidential wannabe John Edwards and the child born to his former mistress. Holy smokes, thank goodness Cleveland did not have to deal with cable news and bloggers back in his day. Good thing for Cleveland he never had to take a seat in the *No Spin Zone*. The guys on FOX would have killed him. Despite the ferocity of modern news reporting, the 19th century reporters still had a field day with the story.

By all accounts, everyone assumed the scandal would sink Cleveland's campaign. Certainly, the story would have ruined his career if he had reacted to the scandal in the way most politicians deal with these sorts of things. This time, think Gary Hart challenging reporters to follow him or Bill Clinton's "I did not have sex with that woman." Deny and deflect is the standard method that politicians deal with personal scandals. If Cleveland had not been Cleveland he might have approached this potential scandal with deny, deny, and deny that anything happened. Instead, *Grover the Good* told his campaign staff that they needed to respond in only one way when questioned about the paternity of Ms. Halpin's son. Cleveland told them to tell the truth. And that is what they did.

The Cleveland campaign freely admitted that the candidate had indeed fathered Ms. Halpin's child. Cleveland admitted, "I am not sure that the baby was mine, but I knew I should do the honorable thing, and have supported the child since his birth."

What?

Insert forehead slap here! The press had no idea how to deal with a scandal when the person involved freely confessed and then conceded that they had been doing the honorable thing since the beginning.

Grover the Good Mustache

Much to the chagrin of his political opponents, the so-called scandal actually benefitted Cleveland's campaign. People viewed him even more favorably than they had before.

Sure, Cleveland made a mistake, but he did the honorable thing by supporting the child the voters were told. Of course, Victorian America may have recognized that this was indeed a private matter, and since Grover had behaved as a gentleman there was no issue.

Of course, the *Killer History* truth is not quite as neat and clean as how the history books report the circumstances of Cleveland's election. Historian Charles Lachman claims Cleveland's real actions in the Halpin scandal make John Edwards look like a choirboy. Lachman's research indicates that Cleveland may have actually raped Halpin, took the boy away from her to be raised by his associates, and sullied her reputation in order to protect his political career.

Since Cleveland followed the scandal-ridden Grant Administration, the public was more than ready for a president that represented truth and honesty. The public was even ready to overlook Cleveland's marriage to 21-year-old Francs Folsum during his first term in the White House. Not only was Cleveland 28 years older than Miss Folsum, but he was also her legal guardian. Fortunately for Cleveland, he did not have to tussle over the custody of his wife with Mia Farrow.

In 1886, at the age of 49, Cleveland married 21-year-old Frances Folsom, his adopted niece

Grover's Rules

Each American presidential administration sets the rules for what is considered proper etiquette during their White House. For example, the George W. Bush administration, in an effort to correct the casual Friday mindset of the Clinton White House, instituted a coat and tie dress code. Of course, Dick Cheney publically noted that as Vice President, he was not part of the executive branch and White House rules did not apply to him. We have no confirmed reports, though, that Cheney showed up to cabinet meetings in a wife beater and flip-flops.

Grover Cleveland and his cabinet

The White House rules are a strong indicator of the acceptable social standards of their time. President Grover Cleveland's 1887 White House rules reflect Victorian social norms. Here are a few samples from Cleveland's rulebook:

- *A gentleman should not bow from a window to a lady, but if a lady recognizes him from a window, he should* return the salutation. It is best, however, for a lady to avoid such recognitions. It is not in the best taste for her to sit sufficiently near her windows to be recognized and be recognized by those passing on the streets.

- *Cleanliness is the outward sign of inward purity. It is not to be supposed that a lady washes to become clean but simply to remain clean.*

- *To the fellows: Do not indulge in long hair, thinking it gives you an artistic look. Except in painters and poets, flowing locks are a ridiculous affection.*

Pretty heavy stuff coming from a dude that married his 'niece'! Oh well, I did get a haircut last week.

Commander-in-Chief and Head Traffic Cop

Woodrow Wilson waves to the crowd during his inauguration

As the previous pages have revealed, presidents, world leaders, and other historical figures can be downright quirky, and this description certainly applies to President Woodrow Wilson.

Thanks to Henry Ford's invention of the assembly line, by the time of Wilson's swearing in as president in 1913, there were already millions of automobiles on the road. Wilson was so hooked on his car that he often spent several hours a day motoring around Washington in order to 'clear his head'.

Advertisement for the Ford Model 'T'

Woodrow Wilson was a car guy, which of course on its own does not make one quirky. However, unlike other car guys who thrive on the adrenalin rush of a fast cars and the thrill of speed, Wilson liked to take things slow. A 1916 issue of Northwest Motorist described Wilson's driving habits, noting that he "lacks the speed mania and prefers an appreciative passage through pleasant country scenes to the thrill that comes from speeding." To enhance his driving experience, Wilson was an early proponent of a national highway system and advocated federal funding for quality road construction.

In addition to bad roads, early automobile travelers faced the challenge of the lack of traffic laws and enforcement. President Wilson's obsession with speed demons began after he suffered a debilitating stroke in 1919. While out on his daily drives, he ordered his chauffeur never to exceed a speed of 15 to 20 miles an hour. Anything faster, Wilson reasoned, was just plain reckless. While the presidential motorcade was crawling along at a snail's pace, from the backseat Wilson freaked out every time another motorist passed his car. This prompted him to order the Secret Service, traveling in the car behind him, to chase down the offending speeder, or as he described them, the public menace. Imagine if you will, a honking motorist passing the presidential motorcade and flipping off the president as they drove by.

Wilson on patrol for speeders

The Secret Service detail was to bring the speeder back so they could receive the presidential tongue lashing that they so deserved. Oddly, the Secret Service was never able to catch up with the speed demons that passed the presidential motorcade.

Wilson's obsession with speeders continued, and this led him to petition the Attorney General concerning his presidential authority to arrest speeders and serve up justice curbside. After much conversation, the Secret Service successfully convinced Wilson that it was not a good idea for the president of the United States to get involved in enforcing traffic statutes. Not only was it dangerous, but they argued it could be humiliating to his office. Having been freed from this important public safety obligation, Wilson was then able to concentrate on the presidential business at hand, which included the Versailles Peace Conference of 1919, and his push for the League of Nations.

Unladylike Tactics

Alice Paul was a woman ahead of her time. She was a radical suffragette and did not hesitate to push the status quo, even if that meant stepping on the toes of senior activists that had been fighting the good fight for women's rights long before she was born.

Paul was educated at Swarthmore and the University of Pennsylvania. Like Susan B. Anthony and earlier activists who challenged the idea of equality for women, she was also a Quaker. However, the similarities between Paul and the earlier activists end with their socio-economic backgrounds and religious upbringings.

Alice Paul

Alice Paul felt that Carrie Chapman Catt's National American Woman Suffrage Association was too pedestrian in their approach, so she sought a more radical and aggressive reaction to the fight for women's rights. While Catt sought a more passive approach to the issue, Paul recognized the power of the new media, moving pictures, and the growing popularity of the national press. She sought out big splashy events that would provoke the authorities and shed much needed light on the cause. She formed the National Woman's Party and decided to focus all of her attention on Woodrow Wilson, who did not support the women's suffrage amendment.

Alice Paul disrupting Wilson's inauguration

She continually sought out ways to annoy Wilson, to shame the president, and to make his life uncomfortable. If you have read the previous *Killer History* story, we have no known examples of Alice Paul driving her car fast, which would have really pissed off Wilson, but, nonetheless, she certainly found ways to get under his skin.

Paul often found herself in direct conflict with the authorities. On the eve of President Wilson's first inaugural parade, Paul organized a suffrage parade of 5,000 women marchers. The parade drew large crowds, and as it progressed some in the crowd grew violent. Many of the marchers were injured, while the police stood by and did nothing to stop the attacks. Nonetheless, the event was covered by every national newspaper and put a damper on Wilson's inaugural activities.

Paul's next step was to ensure the White House was constantly picketed with banners and posters calling on the president to support the vote for women. These women were at first ignored, then harassed, and finally arrested. Some chained themselves to the White House fence. The Suffragettes were thrown into jail, where many of them subsequently took up hunger strikes in order to publicize their cause. Alice Paul herself was force fed and threatened with being committed to an asylum. Of course, the conservative media found it shocking that these educated girls from good families could do these types of things. Conversely, more liberal media outlets publicized the mistreatment of the young women at the hands of the government.

Alice Paul and the Suffragettes were a distraction for President Wilson, who described Alice Paul's' tactics as 'unladylike'. In the end, though faced with increased pressure, Wilson had no other choice but to support the 19th Amendment giving American women the opportunity to express their citizenship rights and vote.

The First Black President?

On January 20, 2009, Barack Obama became the first African American to be elected president of the United States of America. On the other hand, should we believe the conspiracy theorists? I don't mean the conspiracy theorists that believe Obama was born in Kenya! I mean the conspiracy that Americans unknowingly elected its first black president in 1920 with the election of Republican Warren G. Harding!

Warren G. Harding telling you how he rolls

Finding the truth about Harding's ancestry is complicated and the story is framed in rumor and innuendo. The hype about Harding's ethnicity may essentially boil down to American political partisanship at its worst.

Think of the race issue as a 1920 Swift Boat campaign against Harding, which allows us to put his election into perspective. The Ku Klux Klan was at its height of popularity. The Great Migration of African Americans from the rural south to the urban north was in full swing and the nation was only a couple of decades removed from the legal sanction of segregation in the 1896 Plessey v. Ferguson case. Black Codes in the south controlled and limited the actions of black citizens, and lynchings were common all over the nation. It would seem that the easiest way to derail a political campaign in 1920 would be the mere hint that a candidate was black.

Warren G. Harding at 17

The rumors of Harding's black ancestry were credited to Democratic activist William Chancellor; his research on Harding is biased, to say the least. Chancellor's effort to derail the Harding campaign make current efforts to portray Bill Clinton's womanizing or George Bush's National Guard service look small and insignificant. Chancellor was making the point that Harding was a black man based on the legacy rule that only one drop of blood made a person black. Furthermore, Chancellor wanted to prove that only white men were qualified for the presidency and

Harding's blackness disqualified him from the nation's highest office.

So was Warren G. Harding a black man?

This is a good question and not an easy one to answer. We do know Harding never identified as black or of mixed race, although it is highly unlikely that an aspiring politician would openly admit this, even if it was true. He did try very hard to skirt the race issue when confronted in the 1920 election. The New York Times in a 2008 article discovered that Harding's great grandfather admitted that someone tried to discredit him by making the accusation the family was black.

Harding's future father-in-law, Amos Kling, also may have contributed to the rumor when he opposed Harding's marriage to his daughter. Kling tried to discredit Harding by publically using the 'N' word when describing Harding. We also know that once Harding achieved a level of success Kling acquiesced and became one his biggest supporters. Additionally, Harding was described at the time as having a dark complexion and Romanesque features. Of course others described Harding as looking 'presidential'! So who really knows what to think?

Presiding While Drunk

Should there be a breathalyzer test before being sworn in as president of the United States?

Richard M. Nixon, aka Tipsy Dickie

Now we are certainly not assuming that every resident of 1600 Pennsylvania Avenue was a choirboy. A great many of the chief executives have enjoyed a cocktail or some other adult beverage. Given the stress of the job, who could blame the president for tipping a few back when things get a little heated? What most of us do expect is for our chief executive to know his or her limits and to exercise moderation.

Given his proclivity for taping everything that went on in his oval office, we have a wealth of information about Richard Milhous Nixon's consumption habits. Along with his creative audio editing skills, Tricky Dickie knew how to party, or perhaps we should call him Tipsy Dickie?

In 1973, Secretary of State Henry Kissinger told Brent Scowcroft, Deputy of National Security, that Nixon was too loaded to speak with the British prime minister. Kissinger advised Scowcroft, to tell the British PM that the President of the United States would be unavailable until the morning.

Tipsy Dickie toasting Chinese Premier Zhou Enlai

On another occasion, Nixon's drinking almost started World War III. After imbibing a few too many highballs, Nixon's staff informed him that North Korea had shot down a spy plane. Tipsy Dickie ordered preparations for a nuclear attack, which could have led to terrible results. Just getting the missiles out of the silos would have triggered some sort or Dr. Strangelove reaction from the Soviets, and may very well have started World War III. Fortunately, the White House staff did not follow his orders.

1968 Nixon campaign poster

Historian Stephen Ambrose notes that Nixon's drinking really ramped up during the Watergate crisis, which of course makes sense. Many of his oval office recordings reveal his slurred speech and profanity-laced tirades. Nixon certainly exhibited the paranoid behavior of an alcoholic. There is also evidence that he may have been a drug abuser.

Nixon used Dilantin during his presidency, the side effects of which are significant, including slurred speech and mental confusion. In fact, his behavior was so erratic that Secretary of Defense James Schlesinger ordered military commanders not to react to White House orders without first clearing them through his office.

A transcript of the recording between Nixon and Art Linkletter revealed Nixon's conclusion about the difference between drug abusers and drinkers boils down to a single distinction: According to Nixon, drug abusers use drugs to get high and drinkers drink to be social. After a heated exchange, Linkletter and Nixon agreed that drug-induced societies fall apart due to their lack of discipline and motivation.

Nixon said, "At least with liquor, I don't lose motivation." In the interview transcripts, Tipsy Dickie then mumbled something about recently having too much drink, and how this caused him to have conversations with the artwork in the White House.

Afterward

I hope you have enjoyed the previous pages of this small collection. For me, history is always a personal reflection, which allows us to see more clearly how the events of the past unfold. I suspect most people often forget that historical figures were human beings, and the knee jerk reaction is to put these individuals on historical pedestals. There is a real danger in this action as it filters the past through the present. Our present day notions of political correctness and our own biases can influence how we interpret the past. We run the risk of changing the meaning of the great events that shaped the past.

In a recent class discussion, my students and I explored a hallmark of the American national identity, Thomas Jefferson's famous words from the Declaration of Independence.

We hold these truths to be self-evident, that all men are created equal, that they are endowed by the Creator with certain unalienable Rights, that among these are Life, Liberty, and the Pursuit of Happiness.

Of course, it is understood that Thomas Jefferson wrote these words while he also possessed 650 slaves. I would be remiss not to mention that the Declaration of Independence left out the ladies, as Abigail Adams implored her husband John not to forget in 1776.

Despite the obvious contradictions, I was a bit stunned that a student chose to overlook Jefferson's slave ownership because her historical memory reassured her that he was a kind and merciful slaveholder that treated his slaves better than his contemporaries. I should note, she read that assessment on some history buff's website, and of course everything on the internet has got to be true.

Her classmates of course pushed back on her argument noting the hypocrisy of Jefferson's position. Being treated well as a slave was not the same as being treated like a free person. Another student noted that women were not included in the statement. I added that Jefferson only felt property owners should be allowed to vote, so in his mind not even all white men were equal.

To these arguments, the student decried that we were defaming the reputation of a great man and admonished us for manipulating the past. To her discussion post, I replied:

I think the important word is 'man.' Thomas Jefferson was a man, he was not a saint. I tend to have a real problem with putting the founding fathers (ok I also don't like the sexist language of founding fathers either) on pedestals. They were ordinary men that were in the right place at the right time, and did amazing things. Jefferson owned slaves, Washington liked the ladies, John Adams was crabby, Ben Franklin really liked the ladies, Alexander Hamilton was a back stabber, and there are many more examples. One of the real dangers of overlooking that these gentlemen were human is that it discounts the greatness they achieved.

It is easy for a saint to do saintly things, but when a mere mortal performs saintly deeds well that is truly impressive!

Americans only have to look to our Latin American neighbors to the south and their revolving doors of political instability to understand how truly blessed this country has been. In the 18th century, a group of wealthy, white men came together and did something truly miraculous in the course of human history. They created a pretty cool system of government, which has operated fairly efficiently for over 230 years. They were able to put aside personal differences, political aspirations, and their own greed to do what was best for the country.

May the politicians of the next 200 years be equally as great!

"LIBERAL" GRATITUDE.

Now that the good Ship Union has safely passed through the Sea of Trouble into peaceful Waters, shall the Helmsman be thrown overboard?

About the author

Marek McKenna has made history fun and entertaining for students for the past decade. He is a graduate of the University of Iowa and lives in the woods of North Carolina with his co-conspirator Kim and dog Elliot. He facilitates undergraduate history courses at the University of Phoenix. You can find him online at:

http://killerhistory.com

http://marekmckenna.com
http://www.youtube.com/killerhistory.

Follow him on http://twitter.com/killerhistory.

www.ingramcontent.com/pod-product-compliance
Lightning Source LLC
Chambersburg PA
CBHW071546040426
42452CB00008B/1100